Discord

GRAPHIC CAREERS

WAR
CORRESPONDENTS

by Rob Shone

illustrated by Chris Forsey

rosen publishing's
rosen
central

New York

Published in 2008 by The Rosen Publishing Group, Inc.
29 East 21st Street, New York, NY 10010

First edition, 2008

Designed and produced by
David West Books

Editor: Gail Bushnell

Photo credits:
P4b, Roger Fenton; 5t, Ellis Ashmead-Bartlett; 5b, U.S. Marine Corps; 6t, CNN; 6b, U.S. Army; 7b, Jeffrey Russell/U.S. Navy; 44/45, CNN; 45l, Martin Hagberg; 45r,Tech. Sgt. Sean P. Houlihan/USAF.

  Library of Congress Cataloging-in-Publication Data

Shone, Rob.
  War correspondents / by Rob Shone ; illustrated by Chris Forsey. --
1st ed.
      p. cm. -- (Graphic careers)
  Includes index.
  ISBN 978-1-4042-1449-1 (library binding) -- ISBN 978-1-4042-1450-7
(pbk.) -- ISBN 978-1-4042-1451-4 (6 pack)
  1. War correspondents--United States--Biography--Juvenile
literature. 2. Pyle, Ernie, 1900-1945--Juvenile literature. 3.
Schanberg, Sydney H. (Sydney Hillel), 1934---Juvenile literature. 4.
Adie, Kate--Juvenile literature. I. Forsey, Christopher. II. Title.
  PN4871.S54 2008
  070.4'3330922--dc22
  [B]
                                    2007045936

Manufactured in China

CONTENTS

WAR REPORTING FROM THE PAST

Whenever there are major wars, the number of newspapers sold and of people who watch television news programs increases. War correspondents keep the newspapers and television stations supplied with frontline news.

THE GREEK WARS

In 431 BCE the Greek cities of Athens and Sparta began a war that lasted twenty-seven years. We know about the war because an Athenian general, Thucydides, wrote about it. Histories had been written of earlier Greek wars, but this was the first to be reported as it happened, just as modern war reporters do. Thucydides was exiled in 424 BCE by the Athenians. He visited Sparta and so was able to write about the war from their side, too.

Thucydides reported on the war from both the Athenian and the Spartan points of view.

THE FIRST WAR REPORTER

One of the first modern war correspondents was Irishman William Howard Russell. He wrote articles for *The Times* of London on the Crimean War (1853–1856) between Russia and Great Britain, France, and Turkey. Russell described what he saw—the heroic bravery of the soldiers and the corruption and incompetence of the British officers. His reports forced Britain to change the way its army was organized.

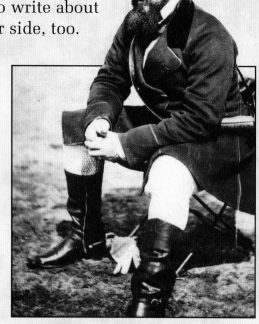

In 1882, Russell retired as a war correspondent. He was made a knight in 1895 and died in 1907.

JOURNALISM AND WORLD WAR

During World War I (1914–1918), the use of machine guns against soldiers advancing on foot led to huge losses. Governments, fearing the loss of support for the war at home, ordered war correspondents to keep bad news from the public. Defeats were reported as though they were victories. When World War II (1939–1945) began, journalists applied to the Allied Forces to become official war correspondents. This official status gave them access to information that they would not usually have had.

British soldiers on the SS Nile, *are bound for the Gallipoli peninsula in Turkey, in 1915.*

Photography can be as important as reporting during wars. Photographers take a break during the Battle of Normandy, France, in 1944.

WARFARE BROUGHT TO THE LIVING ROOM

By 1965 and the start of the Vietnam War, the television networks had new portable and lightweight film cameras. Film crews and reporters were free to go where they wanted. Within two days of being shot, film could be shown on the television evening news. Watching the often harrowing footage helped turn public opinion against the war.

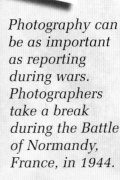

Veteran reporter Walter Cronkite (above) covered the Vietnam War for CBS News. His war reports had a great influence on public opinion in America.

NEWS FROM THE BATTLEFIELD

When Ernie Pyle joined World War II as an official war correspondent he had a simple idea. He would join a unit of soldiers, live with them for a week or two, and then go away and write about the experience. He was the first embedded journalist.

War correspondents often have to deal with heavily armed gunmen. Gaining the trust of these dangerous people is important in order to work safely.

THE EMBEDDED JOURNALIST

After the First Gulf War (1991), journalists complained that the coalition forces had stopped them from doing their job properly. Their only information on the fighting came from the military. In 2003, when a second coalition force was formed to fight in the Persian Gulf, the military decided to attach journalists to fighting units. Their reports were still censored, but this time they could witness the fighting firsthand.

Embedded journalists share the same hardships as the soldiers with whom they are attached.

This is the newsroom of CNN (Cable News Network). CNN was the first network to offer 24-hour television news coverage.

SENDING BACK THE NEWS

When William Howard Russell wrote an article from the Crimea, it took several weeks to reach London and *The Times*. Now, war correspondents can send their stories back to their newspapers or television stations in a matter of seconds. In 1991, during the first Gulf War, the equipment available to send instant reports was not easily portable and could not work without a power source or an electrical generator. Reporters can now carry little more than a cell phone and a battery-powered laptop computer. Film and sound, edited on the laptop, can be sent using the phone and beamed directly into homes.

Some satellite phones, like this Inmarsat system, can be used anywhere in the world. Broadcast-quality words and pictures can be sent directly to the television station.

ERNIE PYLE
—— WORLD WAR II ——
THE WORM'S-EYE POINT OF VIEW

ITALY, DECEMBER 18, 1943. CAPTAIN WASKOW'S BODY HAD BEEN LYING ON THE TOP OF HILL 1205 FOR THREE DAYS.

MEN FROM WASKOW'S COMPANY, THE 143RD INFANTRY, HAD BEEN TRYING TO CLEAR THE MOUNTAIN OF GERMAN FORCES SINCE DECEMBER 8.

ON DECEMBER 15, THE CAPTAIN HAD BEEN HIT BY SHRAPNEL AND KILLED. ONLY NOW COULD HIS BODY BE SAFELY RECOVERED.

THE CAPTAIN'S MEN HAD BEEN WAITING AT THE BOTTOM OF THE MOUNTAIN TRAIL.

ONE BY ONE THEY WENT OVER TO THE BODY.

I'M SORRY, OLD MAN.

WATCHING AND WAITING WITH THE CAPTAIN'S MEN WAS THE JOURNALIST ERNIE PYLE...

...HE HAD FOUND ANOTHER STORY.

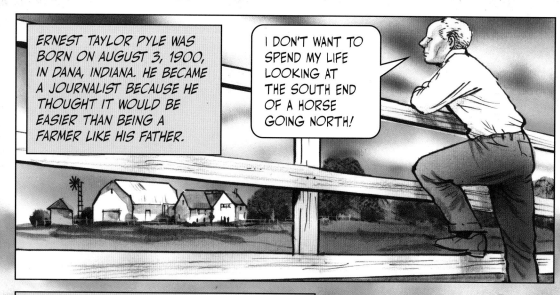

ERNEST TAYLOR PYLE WAS BORN ON AUGUST 3, 1900, IN DANA, INDIANA. HE BECAME A JOURNALIST BECAUSE HE THOUGHT IT WOULD BE EASIER THAN BEING A FARMER LIKE HIS FATHER.

I DON'T WANT TO SPEND MY LIFE LOOKING AT THE SOUTH END OF A HORSE GOING NORTH!

SINCE 1935 HE HAD BEEN TRAVELING AROUND THE COUNTRY AS A ROVING REPORTER.

HE WAS DOING WHAT HE ENJOYED THE BEST—VISITING PLACES, MEETING PEOPLE, AND WRITING ABOUT THEM.

HE WROTE 1,000 WORDS A STORY, SIX STORIES A WEEK. READERS LIKED HIS EASYGOING WRITING STYLE.

IN 1939, WAR BROKE OUT IN EUROPE. ERNIE PYLE WENT TO ENGLAND. HE WAS IN LONDON DURING THE BLITZ* OF 1940. PYLE WROTE, "I DOUBT IF YOU HAVE EVER SEEN THE WHOLE HORIZON OF A CITY LINED WITH GREAT FIRES—SCORES OF THEM, PERHAPS HUNDREDS."

IN DECEMBER 1941, AMERICA ENTERED THE WAR. ERNIE PYLE WAS SENT TO NORTH AFRICA AS A WAR CORRESPONDENT FOR SCRIPPS-HOWARD NEWSPAPER ALLIANCE. AT FIRST HE WROTE ABOUT THE STRATEGIES AND TACTICS OF THE WAR. BUT THEN, ON HIS WAY TO A PRESS BRIEFING...

STUKAS!

*THE BLITZ (SHORT FOR BLITZKRIEG OR LIGHTNING WAR) WAS THE NAME GIVEN TO THE NIGHTLY GERMAN AIR RAIDS OVER LONDON DURING 1940 AND 1941.

THE GERMAN STUKA DIVE BOMBERS ATTACKED THE AIRFIELD.

GET IN THE FOXHOLE!

WHEN THE ATTACK WAS OVER...

WHEW! THAT WAS CLOSE!

PYLE'S COMPANION IN THE FOXHOLE WAS DEAD.

BACK IN HIS TENT, PYLE BROODED ABOUT WHAT HAD HAPPENED. INSTEAD OF AN ARTICLE ON THE BRIEFING, HE DECIDED TO WRITE ABOUT THE DEAD SOLDIER IN THE DITCH.

FROM THAT DAY ON PYLE WROTE ABOUT THE ORDINARY SOLDIER. HE CALLED IT THE "WORM'S-EYE POINT OF VIEW."

HE WOULD SPEND A FEW DAYS WITH A COMBAT UNIT, NO MATTER HOW DANGEROUS IT WAS, LIVING AS THE UNIT DID. LATER ON, AWAY FROM THE FIGHTING, HE WOULD WRITE ABOUT THE EXPERIENCE. THE MEN LIKED HIM. HE WAS THE ONLY JOURNALIST WHO WAS INTERESTED IN WHAT THEY HAD TO SAY.

ERNIE PYLE USED THIS METHOD OF REPORTING THROUGHOUT THE NORTH AFRICA CAMPAIGN...

...THE INVASION OF SICILY IN JULY 1943...

...AND THE PUSH THROUGH ITALY. IN THE THREE MONTHS FROM SEPTEMBER TO DECEMBER, THE GERMAN ARMY HAD BEEN DRIVEN BACK TO A DEFENSIVE LINE 90 MILES (144 KILOMETERS) FROM ROME, A LINE THAT INCLUDED HILL 1205.

FROM HILL 1205, PYLE WENT TO THE FIFTH ARMY REST CENTER TO WRITE UP HIS STORIES. DON WHITEHEAD, A FRIEND AND FELLOW WAR REPORTER, WAS ALSO THERE.

HI, ERNIE. YOU LOOK GLUM. WHAT'S WRONG?

OH, I DON'T KNOW, DON. I'VE LOST THE TOUCH. THIS STUFF STINKS. I JUST CAN'T SEEM TO GET GOING AGAIN.

HERE, YOU LOOK AT IT. TELL ME WHAT YOU THINK.

"IN THIS WAR I HAVE KNOWN A LOT OF OFFICERS WHO WERE LOVED AND RESPECTED BY THE SOLDIERS UNDER THEM..."

"...BUT NEVER HAVE I CROSSED THE TRAIL OF ANY MAN AS BELOVED AS CAPTAIN HENRY T. WASKOW OF BELTON, TEXAS."

DON WHITEHEAD FINISHED READING THE PIECE.

ERNIE, IF THIS IS A SAMPLE FROM A GUY WHO'S LOST HIS TOUCH...

...THEN THE REST OF US HAD BETTER GO HOME!

ON JANUARY 10, 1944, THE WASHINGTON DAILY NEWS DEVOTED THE ENTIRE FRONT PAGE TO THE WASKOW ARTICLE. ANOTHER 200 NEWSPAPERS PRINTED IT, AND IT WAS READ ON RADIO PROGRAMS.

"...HE CARRIED IN HIM A SINCERITY AND A GENTLENESS THAT MADE PEOPLE WANT TO BE GUIDED BY HIM..."

"...'AFTER MY OWN FATHER, HE CAME NEXT,' A SERGEANT TOLD ME. 'HE ALWAYS LOOKED AFTER US,' A SOLDIER SAID..."

"...DEAD MEN HAD BEEN COMING DOWN THE MOUNTAIN ALL EVENING, LASHED ONTO THE BACKS OF MULES..."

...'THIS ONE IS CAPTAIN WASKOW,' ONE OF THEM SAID QUIETLY..."

16

"...ANOTHER MAN CAME; I THINK HE WAS AN OFFICER. IT WAS HARD TO TELL OFFICERS FROM MEN IN THE HALFLIGHT..."

"...THE MAN LOOKED DOWN INTO THE DEAD CAPTAIN'S FACE, AND THEN HE SPOKE DIRECTLY TO HIM, AS THOUGH HE WERE ALIVE. HE SAID: 'I'M SORRY, OLD MAN'..."

"...AND GENTLY STRAIGHTENED THE POINTS OF THE CAPTAIN'S SHIRT COLLAR..."

"...AND THEN HE GOT UP AND WALKED AWAY DOWN THE ROAD IN THE MOONLIGHT, ALL ALONE."

THE MOVING STORY, SIMPLY TOLD, HAD TOUCHED AMERICAN HEARTS. THOUSANDS OF LETTERS OF SYMPATHY WERE SENT TO THE WASKOW FAMILY. AND THE ARTICLE HAD MADE ERNIE PYLE FAMOUS.

ON JUNE 6, 1944, AN ALLIED INVASION FORCE SET OFF FROM ENGLAND AND LANDED ON THE NORMANDY BEACHES OF FRANCE.

ERNIE PYLE ARRIVED THE NEXT DAY. BY THE TWELFTH, THE AMERICAN PUBLIC WAS READING ABOUT THE THINGS HE SAW.

LOOK AT ALL THIS STUFF! HUMAN LITTER!

LIFE PRESERVERS, SOCKS, SHOES, DIARIES, SEWING KITS, PHOTOGRAPHS, RAZORS, POCKETBOOKS, WRITING PAPER—IT'S LIKE A HIGH-WATER MARK.

THERE'S ENOUGH EQUIPMENT HERE TO START A SMALL WAR!

STILL, WE CAN AFFORD IT.

LATER.

GERMAN PRISONERS!

KEEP MOVING!

WHAT ARE THEY LOOKING AT?

FROM THE NORMANDY BEACHES, PYLE AND THE ALLIED ARMIES MOVED INLAND.

OFFICERS LIKED ERNIE PYLE AS MUCH AS THE ORDINARY SOLDIERS DID. THEY BELIEVED HE WAS GOOD FOR MORALE. TWO OF HIS ADMIRERS WERE GENERAL BRADLEY AND GENERAL EISENHOWER, THE LEADERS OF THE AMERICAN FORCES.

THE MEN ALWAYS FIGHT HARDER WHEN YOU'RE AROUND, ERNIE.

IT'S GOOD OF YOU TO SAY SO, GENERAL EISENHOWER, SIR.

ON AUGUST 25, 1944, PARIS WAS LIBERATED FROM THE GERMANS. PYLE REPORTED FROM THE CITY. HIS HEALTH WAS SUFFERING, THOUGH. IN SEPTEMBER, HE LEFT EUROPE FOR HOME.

WHILE HE WAS BACK HOME, PYLE RECEIVED AWARDS FROM THE UNIVERSITIES OF NEW MEXICO AND INDIANA. HE WAS ALSO AWARDED THE PULITZER PRIZE* FOR HIS 1943 WAR REPORTS.

ROBERT MITCHUM

BURGESS MEREDITH

ERNIE PYLE'S

THE STORY OF G.I. JOE

Directed by WILLIAM A. WELLMAN

*A YEARLY PRIZE AWARDED TO THE BEST OF AMERICAN JOURNALISM, LITERATURE, AND MUSIC. IT WAS FOUNDED IN 1917 BY JOSEPH PULITZER, A NEWSPAPER PUBLISHER.

HOLLYWOOD HAD TAKEN AN INTEREST IN PYLE, TOO. A FEATURE FILM, "THE STORY OF G.I. JOE," WAS MADE. IT WAS BASED ON PYLE'S ARTICLES ABOUT THE FIGHTING IN ITALY AND ON THE STORY OF CAPTAIN WASKOW.

ERNIE PYLE STAYED IN NEW MEXICO UNTIL THE END OF THE YEAR. IN JANUARY 1945, HE WAS IN THE PACIFIC ON BOARD THE USS CABOT, A SMALL AIRCRAFT CARRIER.

ON APRIL 18, PYLE VISITED THE SMALL ISLAND OF IE SHIMA, NEAR THE LARGER PACIFIC ISLAND OF OKINAWA. HE WAS ON HIS WAY TO THE FRONT LINE WHEN...

PYLE AND HIS COMPANION TOOK COVER.

THE MACHINE GUN FIRED AGAIN.

ARE YOU OKAY, ERNIE?

ERNIE!

ERNIE PYLE WAS DEAD. A MACHINE GUN BULLET HAD STRUCK HIM.

BY APRIL 1945, ERNIE PYLE HAD WRITTEN 700,000 WORDS ON THE WAR. HIS COLUMNS WERE PRINTED IN 400 DAILY AND 300 WEEKLY AMERICAN NEWSPAPERS, WHICH WERE READ BY OVER 14,000,000 PEOPLE. NOW MILLIONS MOURNED HIS DEATH. HE HAD WRITTEN ABOUT THE WAR FROM THE VIEWPOINT OF THE ORDINARY SOLDIER. TO THE NEWSPAPER READER, THESE COULD BE STORIES ABOUT THEIR OWN BROTHERS, SONS, FATHERS, AND HUSBANDS FIGHTING IN THE WAR. ERNIE PYLE NEVER GOT TO SEE THE FILM "THE STORY OF G.I. JOE." IT WAS RELEASED TWO MONTHS AFTER HE WAS KILLED.

AT THIS SPOT THE 77TH INFANTRY DIVISION LOST A BUDDY ERNIE PYLE 18 APRIL 1945

THE END

SYDNEY SCHANBERG
—— SOUTHEAST ASIA ——
TRAGEDY IN CAMBODIA

THE AMERICAN B-52 BOMBER OPENED ITS BOMB BAY DOORS
AS IT NEARED THE TARGET. IT WAS AUGUST 7, 1973.

THE BOMBS WERE MEANT FOR THE KHMER ROUGE,
REBELS FIGHTING THE CAMBODIAN GOVERNMENT.

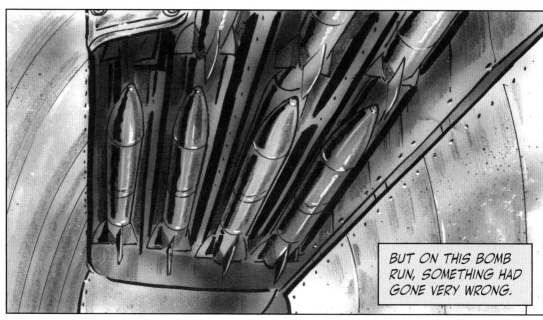

BUT ON THIS BOMB
RUN, SOMETHING HAD
GONE VERY WRONG.

TWENTY TONS (18.1 METRIC TONS) OF BOMBS FELL ON NEAK LEUNG, A MARKET TOWN LOYAL TO THE CAMBODIAN GOVERNMENT.

THE CAMBODIAN CAPITAL, PHNOM PENH, LATER ON THAT DAY. NEW YORK TIMES REPORTER SYDNEY SCHANBERG AND HIS TRANSLATOR, DITH PRAN, WERE ON THEIR WAY TO THE AMERICAN AIR FORCE BASE.

SO LET ME GET THIS STRAIGHT, PRAN. YOU ACTUALLY SAW THE WOUNDED BEING TAKEN OUT OF THE AMBULANCES.

YES, SYDNEY. THERE WERE MANY OF THEM, ALL FROM NEAK LEUNG.

I WAS TOLD THE TOWN HAS BEEN BOMBED.

NEAK LEUNG—THAT'S ABOUT FORTY MILES FROM HERE, ISN'T IT? LET'S HOPE THE MILITARY CAN GET US THERE.

THE U.S. AIR FORCE BASE, PHNOM PENH.

COLONEL! IS IT TRUE? HAS THERE BEEN SOME KIND OF MASS BOMBING IN NEAK LEUNG? CAN YOU GET ME THERE? I'D LIKE TO SEE FOR MYSELF.

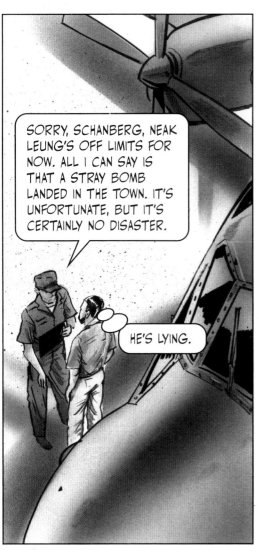

SORRY, SCHANBERG, NEAK LEUNG'S OFF LIMITS FOR NOW. ALL I CAN SAY IS THAT A STRAY BOMB LANDED IN THE TOWN. IT'S UNFORTUNATE, BUT IT'S CERTAINLY NO DISASTER.

HE'S LYING.

LATER, SCHANBERG SPOTTED A FRIEND FROM THE AMERICAN EMBASSY.

HEY, DOUGLAS. COME ON, YOU MUST KNOW WHAT'S GOING ON. WHAT HAPPENED IN NEAK LEUNG?

OKAY, I'LL TELL YOU, BUT DON'T QUOTE ME, RIGHT. A B-52 ACCIDENTALLY DROPPED ITS WHOLE LOAD ON THE TOWN.

WHAT ABOUT CASUALTIES?

TENS, MAYBE HUNDREDS DEAD. WE JUST DON'T KNOW YET.

COME ON, PRAN, WE'VE GOT TO GET THERE.

LEAVE THAT TO ME, SYDNEY.

29

SCHANBERG AND PRAN WALKED THROUGH THE TOWN TALKING TO PEOPLE, TRYING TO FIND OUT WHAT HAD HAPPENED.

HE SAYS HIS WIFE AND FIVE CHILDREN ARE ALL DEAD. HE HAS LOST EVERYTHING.

SUDDENLY...

SYDNEY! GOVERNMENT SOLDIERS! THEY HAVE KHMER ROUGE PRISONERS!

PRAN, THEY'RE GOING TO EXECUTE THEM!

33

SCHANBERG AND PRAN WERE HELD FOR SEVERAL HOURS.

THAKKA THAKKA THAKKA

CHOPPERS!

THAKKA THAKKA THAKKA!

THE MILITARY HAD FLOWN IN THE REST OF THE PRESS.

COLONEL, IS THERE ROOM FOR ME AND PRAN TO HITCH A RIDE BACK TO PHNOM PENH?

YOU GOT HERE ON YOUR OWN. YOU CAN GET BACK ON YOUR OWN.

THE DEAD AND WOUNDED HAD BEEN TAKEN AWAY BEFORE THE PRESS GOT HERE. THE COLONEL SHOWED THEM WHAT HE WANTED THEM TO SEE.

THE ACCIDENT KILLED 137 PEOPLE, AND INJURED 258. SCHANBERG'S REPORT MADE THE FRONT PAGE OF THE NEW YORK TIMES. HIS ARTICLE AND BOOK, "THE DEATH AND LIFE OF DITH PRAN" WAS MADE INTO THE MOVIE, "THE KILLING FIELDS," IN 1984.

THE END

35

Kate Adie
— THE FIRST GULF WAR —
Desert Storm

ON AUGUST 2, 1990, 100,000 SOLDIERS OF THE REPUBLIC OF IRAQ ARMY INVADED THE STATE OF KUWAIT. AFTER TWO DAYS OF FIGHTING, THE IRAQI FORCES HAD OVERTHROWN THEIR TINY NEIGHBOR. THE IRAQIS, LED BY SADDAM HUSSEIN, WANTED TO TAKE CONTROL OF KUWAIT'S RICH OIL FIELDS.

COALITION FORCES WERE FORMED, MADE UP OF SOLDIERS FROM MANY COUNTRIES. IF THE IRAQIS DID NOT LEAVE KUWAIT PEACEFULLY THE COALITION FORCES WERE SET TO DRIVE THEM OUT.

WITH THE COALITION FORCES CAME A SMALL ARMY OF JOURNALISTS, INCLUDING THE BBC'S KATE ADIE. ALL OFFICIAL WAR CORRESPONDENTS WERE ATTACHED TO MILITARY UNITS. THEY BECAME PART OF THE ARMY.

THEY WERE INOCULATED AGAINST DESERT DISEASES...

...HAD TO UNDERGO DRILLS TO GUARD AGAINST CHEMICAL AND BIOLOGICAL ATTACKS...

...AND LIVED THE SAME WAY AS ALL THE OTHER SOLDIERS.

OVER THE NEXT FEW MONTHS, WHILE THE UNITED NATIONS TRIED TO PERSUADE SADDAM HUSSEIN AND HIS TROOPS TO LEAVE KUWAIT, KATE ADIE AND THE REST OF THE BRITISH TELEVISION NEWS POOL BEGAN TO SEND BACK THEIR REPORTS. THEY WATCHED THE STEADY BUILD UP OF EQUIPMENT AT THE AIR BASES AND SAUDI PORTS.

THEY INTERVIEWED SOLDIERS...

...AND JOINED THE ARMY ON EXERCISES.

BACK AT THE BASE, A REPORT WOULD BE TAKEN TO THE FORWARD TRANSMISSION UNIT. THIS WAS A SMALL MOBILE STUDIO. HERE THE FILM COULD BE EDITED AND ADDITIONAL IMAGES AND WORDS ADDED.

USING A SATELLITE DISH, KATE ADIE COULD SEND A FINISHED PACKAGE DIRECTLY TO THE BBC IN LONDON.

A REPORT COULD BE SLOTTED INTO A NEWS PROGRAM, EXACTLY WHEN IT WAS NEEDED.

REPORTING FROM THE PERSIAN GULF IS KATE ADIE.

ON JANUARY 16, 1991, THE DEADLINE FOR SADDAM HUSSEIN TO WITHDRAW HIS TROOPS FROM KUWAIT PASSED. OPERATION DESERT STORM BEGAN. DAY AND NIGHT, FOR THE NEXT FIVE WEEKS, IRAQI MILITARY POSITIONS AND THE IRAQI CAPITAL, BAGHDAD, WERE BOMBED.

ON SUNDAY, FEBRUARY 24, THE GROUND ATTACK STARTED.

40

GAPS HAD BEEN BLASTED IN THE BERM, A DEFENSIVE SAND WALL THAT RAN THE LENGTH OF THE BORDER. THE COALITION FORCES POURED THROUGH THESE HOLES.

AFTER WEEKS OF BOMBARDMENT, IRAQI SOLDIERS WERE HAPPY TO SURRENDER.

MEANWHILE, KATE ADIE HAD MANAGED TO GET A RIDE INTO KUWAIT CITY IN AN ARMY HELICOPTER. BENEATH THEM, HUNDREDS OF KUWAITI OIL WELLS BURNED. THEY HAD BEEN SET ON FIRE BY THE RETREATING IRAQI ARMY.

ON FEBRUARY 28, A CEASE-FIRE WAS ANNOUNCED. THE FOLLOWING DAY, KATE ADIE AND HER TEAM WERE ON A ROAD LEADING FROM KUWAIT CITY TO IRAQ. ON FEBRUARY 26, PART OF THE IRAQI ARMY HAD TRIED TO ESCAPE FROM KUWAIT CITY ALONG THIS ROAD. THEY FLED INTO THE PATH OF AN ONGOING BATTLE.

AT A POLICE STATION ON THE ROAD THE AMERICAN SECOND MARINE DIVISION HAD FOUND IRAQI TANKS.

WE WERE ATTEMPTING TO CUT THE FLEEING FORCES FROM GOING NORTH. BECAUSE THEY WERE DESPERATE THEY FOUGHT FOR SOME TIME.

WHAT WAS THE SCENE LIKE?

WE HAD ARTILLERY EXPLODING, T-55 TANKS EXPLODING, A LOT OF SMALL ARMS FIRE, AND THERE WAS A PILE OF SMOKE FROM THE BURNING FUEL. IT WAS LIKE NIGHTTIME.

EVERY PRIVATE CAR, VAN, AND TRUCK HAD BEEN DRIVEN BY IRAQI SOLDIERS. GUNS AND AMMUNITION SPILLED OUT, ALONG WITH THEIR KUWAITI SOUVENIRS. THE LOOT FROM MONTHS OF OCCUPATION. THE SCENE WAS BOTH DEVASTATING AND PATHETIC.

THIS IS KATE ADIE FOR THE BRITISH TELEVISION NEWS POOL, ON THE ROAD FROM KUWAIT TO IRAQ.

KATE ADIE WENT ON TO COVER THE WAR IN YUGOSLAVIA, THE RWANDAN GENOCIDE, AND THE CONFLICT IN SIERRA LEONE FOR THE BBC. SADDAM HUSSEIN HAD LOST THE WAR AND AGREED WITH ALL THE COALITION DEMANDS. HE WAS DEPOSED IN 2003 BY A SECOND COALITION FORCE.

THE END

HOW TO BECOME A WAR CORRESPONDENT

Many famous journalists from the past had no training but learned their skills on the job. Today young would-be reporters are expected to have attended a journalism program.

QUALIFICATIONS

The first school for journalists was founded in 1908 at the University of Missouri. Now there are hundreds to choose from around the world. Known as j-schools, they can offer students training in practical skills, such as interviewing and research techniques. They can also teach more academic subjects, such as media studies, journalism and ethics, and cultural awareness. In some countries, a post-graduate journalism class is taken after gaining a university degree.

There is no substitute for practical experience when reporting from a war zone.

Newspaper sales increase during a war as readers are eager to discover the latest news.

The production control room in a television studio is also called the gallery. It is here that film footage from a war zone is sent to be broadcast.

GLOSSARY

bombardment A prolonged attack using missiles and bombs.

briefing A meeting with the purpose of giving out information or instructions.

brooded Thought seriously and at length about a subject.

campaign Military operations performed within a set period or given geographical area.

censored Written or visual material that has been officially examined and had unacceptable parts taken out or changed.

coalition A temporary alliance.

devastating Something that is very damaging.

embedded Something that is fixed inside a larger element.

ethics The ideas that determine right from wrong.

execute To carry out a death sentence.

exiled Banned from living in one's own country.

genocide The attempt to kill the members of a whole country or ethnic group.

harrowing Something that causes emotional distress.

incompetence The state of being unable to perform a duty.

inoculated To be protected against disease.

lashed To be tied down with rope.

morale Great confidence and high spirits.

mourned Showed formal and public regret at a death or loss.

pathetic Something that arouses feelings of pity.

roving Traveling from place to place.

scoop A news story the first time it is published or broadcast.

shrapnel The small pieces of metal that are created from a bomb's shell when it explodes.

sincerity Honesty.

souvenir A small object that is bought or taken as a reminder of a place.

strategies Overall plans of action.

Stukas German Junkers Ju-87 dive bombers, or Sturzkampfflugzeug, meaning "diving combat airplane."

tactics The methods by which plans are carried out.

FOR MORE INFORMATION

ORGANIZATIONS

Friends of Journalists for Human Rights USA
6395 Private Road 2604
Argyle, TX 76226
(713) 732-6470
Web site: http://www.jhr.ca/en/#

Indiana University School of Journalism
Ernie Pyle Hall
940 East Seventh Street
Bloomington, IN 47405-7108
(812) 855-9247
Web site: http://www.journalism.indiana.edu

FOR FURTHER READING

Alagna, Magdalena. *War Correspondents: Life Under Fire*. New York, NY: Rosen Publishing, 2003.

Boomhower, Ray E. *The Soldier's Friend: A Life of Ernie Pyle*. Indianapolis, IN: Indiana Historical Society Press, 2006.

Castro, Janet. *Career Opportunities in Journalism*. New York, NY: Facts on File, 2007.

Colman, Penny. *Where the Action Was: Women War Correspondents in World War II*. New York, NY: Crown Publishers, 2002.

Goldberg, Jan. *Careers in Journalism*. Columbus, OH: McGraw Hill, 2005.

Pyle, Ernie. *Here Is Your War: The Story of G.I. Joe*. Lincoln, NE: University of Nebraska Press, 2004.

Schanberg, Sydney H. *The Death and Life of Dith Pran*. New York, NY: Penguin Books, 1985.

INDEX

Web Sites

Due to the changing nature of Internet links, Rosen Publishing has developed an online list of Web sites related to the subject of this book. This site is updated regularly. Please use this link to access the list:

http://www.rosenlinks.com/gc/waco